PIANO • VOCAL • GUITAR

MW00534895

ISBN 978-1-61774-181-4

HAL•LEONARD®
CORPORATION

7777 W. BLUEMOUND RD. P.O. BOX 13819 MILWAUKEE, WI 53213

Visit Hal Leonard Online at
www.halleonard.com

I WANNA BE YOUR LOVER

Words and Music by
PRINCE

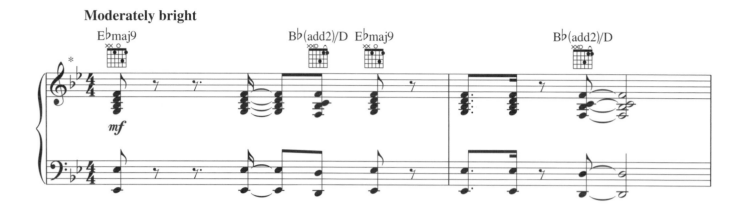

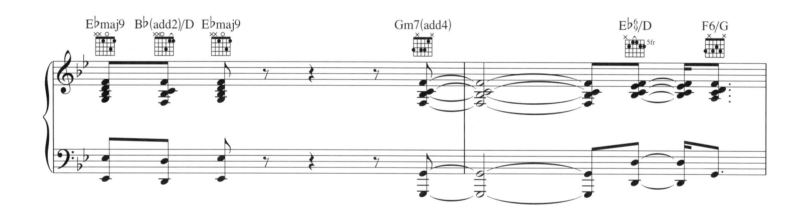

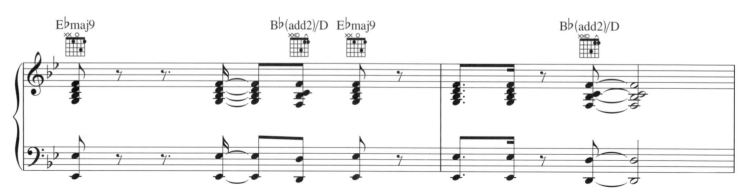

* *Recorded a half step higher.*

UPTOWN

Words and Music by
PRINCE

Moderate Funk

1. She saw me walk-in' down the streets of your fine cit - y.
2. lit - tle girl? I ain't got time 2 play."
3. *(See additional lyrics)*

Additional Lyrics

Soon as we got there, good times a-rollin',
White, Black, Puerto Rican, everybody just a freakin',
Good times a-rollin'.
She started dancin' in the streets,
The girl, she's just gone mad,
She even made love 2 me, the best that I ever had.
I don't usually talk 2 strangers,
But this time it's alright.
She got me hot, I couldn't stop,
Good times a-rollin' all night.

CONTROVERSY

Words and Music by
PRINCE

I just can't be - lieve __ all the things peo - ple say.
I can't un - der - stand __ hu - man cu - ri - os - i - ty.

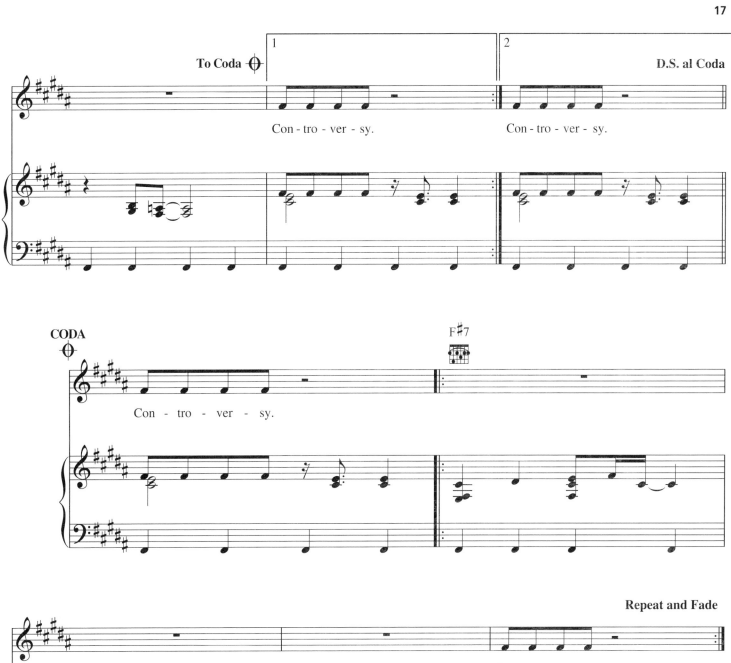

opt. Rap Lyrics

Our Father who art in heaven, hallowed be Thy name.
Thy kingdom come, Thy will be done on earth as it is in heaven.
Give us this day our daily bread and forgive us our trespasses
As we forgive those who trespass against us.
Lead us not into temptation but deliver us from evil,
For Thine is the kingdom and the power and the glory forever and ever.
Controversy.
People call me rude, I wish we all were nude.
I wish there were no black and white,
I wish there were no rules.
Controversy.

1999

Words and Music by
PRINCE

22

DELIRIOUS

Words and Music by
PRINCE

Fast

26

WHEN DOVES CRY

Words and Music by
PRINCE

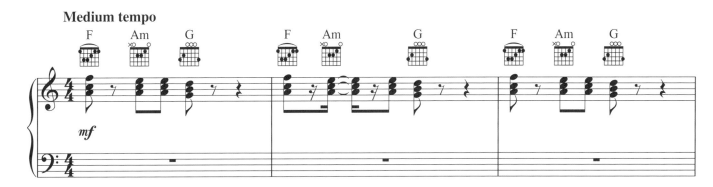

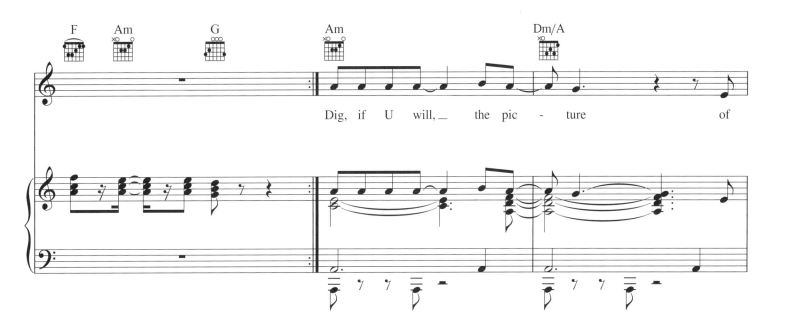

Dig, if U will, __ the pic - ture of

U and I en-gaged in a kiss. The sweat of your bod - y cov -

29

I WOULD DIE 4 U

Words and Music by
PRINCE

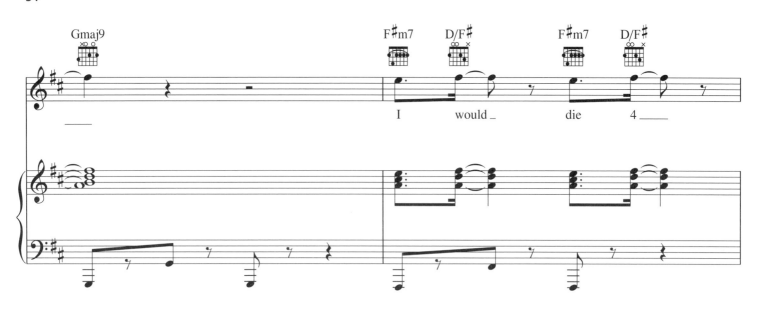

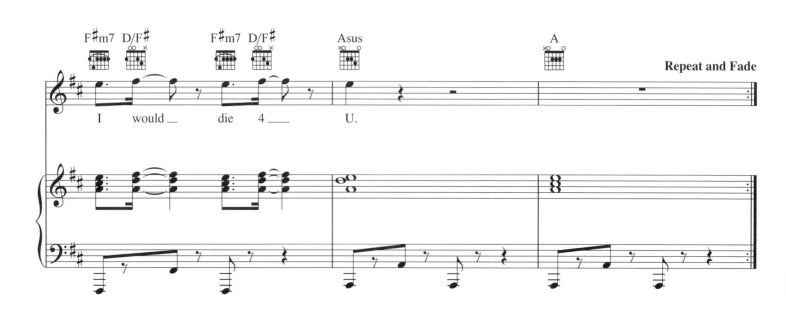

PURPLE RAIN

Words and Music by
PRINCE

Pur - ple rain, pur - ple rain. __

I on - ly want 2 see U, _____ on - ly want 2 see U _____ in the pur - ple rain. __

SIGN O' THE TIMES

Words and Music by
PRINCE

Moderate Funk

Oh yeah, __

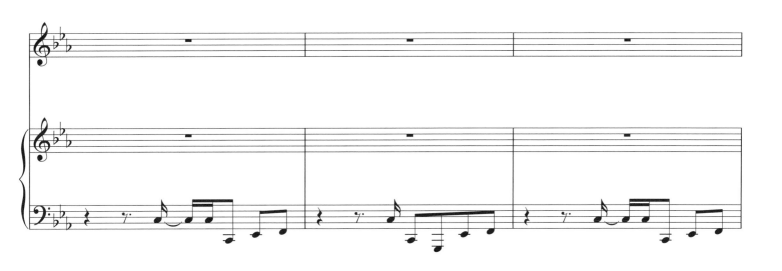

In France __ a skin-ny man died __ of a big dis-ease __

We'll call him Nate   (if it's a boy.)

Time, ___
Time, ___
Guitar solo (on repeat)

time. ___
time. ___

Repeat and Fade

I COULD NEVER TAKE
THE PLACE OF YOUR MAN

Words and Music by
PRINCE

52

ALPHABET STREET

Words and Music by
PRINCE

DIAMONDS AND PEARLS

Words and Music by
PRINCE

GETT OFF

Words and Music by PRINCE
and ARLESTER CHRISTIAN

Moderately, with a heavy beat

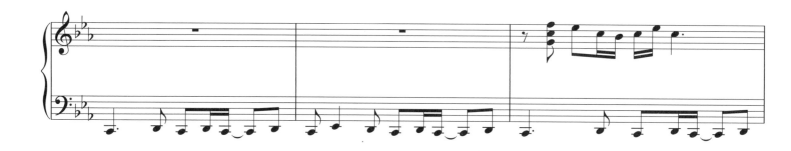

(1., D.S.) How can I put this in a way so as not 2 of-fend or __ un - nerve, __

(2.) I clocked the jizz from a friend of yours named Va - nes-sa Bet. __

but there's a ru-mor go-ing ___ all 'round ___ that U ain't been get-tin' served. ___
She said U told her a fan - ta - sy ___ that got her all wet. ___

They say that U ain't U ___ know what ___ in, ba - by, who knows ___ how long? ___
Some-thing a-bout a lit - tle box ___ with a mir-ror and a tongue in - side. ___

It's hard 4 me 2 say ___ what's right ___ when all ___ I wan - na do is wrong. ___
What she told me then ___ got me ___ so hot, ___ I knew that we could slide. ___   Gett

N.C.

off ___ 2 ___ 3 ___ po - si - tions in a one - night stand.   Gett

- by... here I am.

Rap Lyrics

Oooh I think I like it with the dress half on
I'll zip it far enough 2 see the crack-o'-dawn
Don't worry 'bout the bust, I'm gonna lock up every door
Then we can do it in the kitchen on the floor
Or in the bathroom standing on the tub and holding on the rod
In the closet underneath the clothes and oh, my God
In the bedroom on the dresser with your feet in the drawers
In the pantry on the shelf I guarantee U won't be bored
The pool table, yeah, move the stix and put the 8-ball
Where it's sure 2 stick
Dudley do no wrong 2night if Nell just let him kick it

MONEY DON'T MATTER 2 NIGHT

Words and Music by
PRINCE

One more   card   and it's   2 ___ 2,   un - luck - y   4   him   a - just
Look,   here's   a   cool in - vest - ment,   they're   tell - in' him   he   just
Hey   now,   may - be   we   can   find   a   good   rea - son   2   send a   child   off   2 ___

7

Words and Music by PRINCE,
LOWELL FULSOM and JIMMY McCRACKLIN

Moderately

All 7 and we will watch them __ fall. __ They

stand in the way of love and we will smoke them __ all __ with an in-tel-lect and a

sav-oir - faire. __ No one in the whole u-ni-verse will ev-er com-pare. __

NOTHING COMPARES 2 U

Words and Music by
PRINCE

MY NAME IS PRINCE

Words and Music by PRINCE
and ANTHONY MOSLEY

My name is

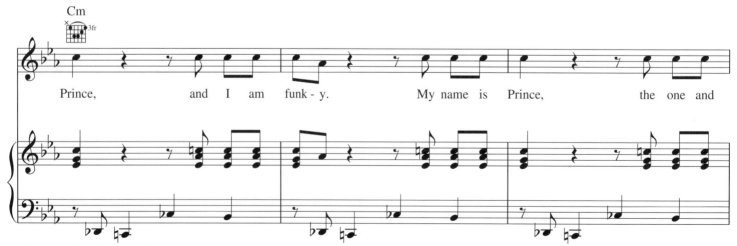

Prince,   and I am funk-y.   My name is Prince,   the one and

Recorded a whole step lower.

on - ly.   I did not come   2 funk a - round;   'til I get your

daugh-ter,   I won't leave this town.   In the be - gin-ning   God made the

Cm

sea,   but on the sev - enth day   He made

me.   He was try-in' 2 rest, y'all,   when He heard this

Rap Lyrics

The funkier I be,
The funkier I get, oh, get, oh.
Lickety split on the lyric,
A new jack in the pulpit.
Watch it, deacon, your track is leakin'.
What is it U're seek-in'?
The syncopated rhymes are at their peak when...

You jumped on, jumped on my dick.
That's one thing I don't play.
The jockstrap was 2 big 4 U anyway.
U're just a simpleton;
I'll bust U like a pimple, son.
My star is 2 bright,
Boy, I'll sink U like the ship Poseidon Adventure.

U're bumpin' dentures to be cocksure.
There must be more comin' from Ur mouth than manure.
So with a flow and a spray, I say hey,
U must become a prince before U're king, anyway.

LET'S GO CRAZY

Words and Music by
PRINCE

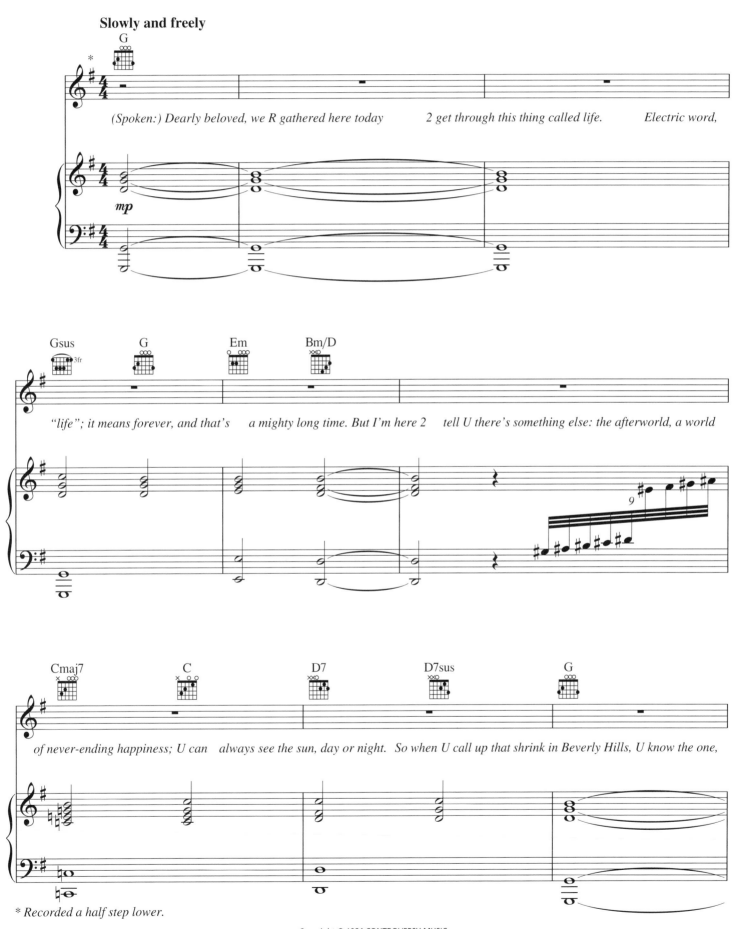

Slowly and freely

(Spoken:) Dearly beloved, we R gathered here today   2 get through this thing called life.   Electric word,

"life"; it means forever, and that's   a mighty long time. But I'm here 2   tell U there's something else: the afterworld, a world

of never-ending happiness; U can   always see the sun, day or night.   So when U call up that shrink in Beverly Hills, U know the one,

* Recorded a half step lower.

he's com - ing.

LITTLE RED CORVETTE

Words and Music by
PRINCE

* *Recorded a half step higher.*

LET'S WORK

Words and Music by
PRINCE

Up Funk feel

Let's   work!

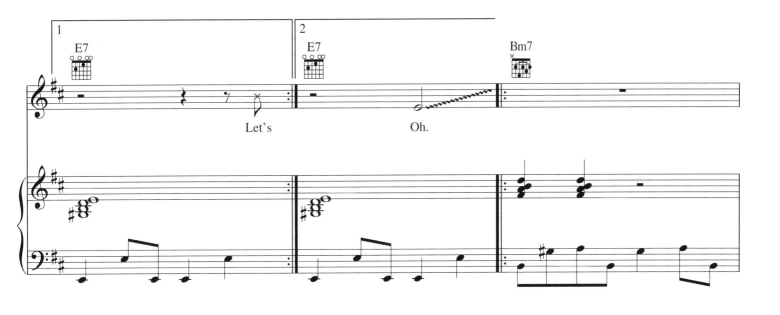

Let's   Oh.

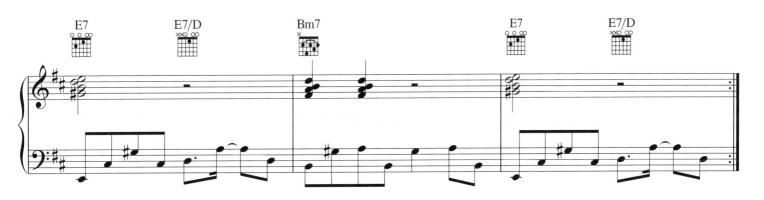

POP LIFE

Words and Music by
PRINCE

Moderately

What's the mat-ter with your life?
What U put-ting in your nose?

Is the pov-er-ty bring-ing you
Is that where all your mon-ey

down?
goes?

Is the mail-man jerk-ing U a-round?
The riv-er of ad-dic-tion flows, *U think* **it's**

Did he

* Recorded a half step higher.

SHE'S ALWAYS IN MY HAIR

Words and Music by
PRINCE

RASPBERRY BERET

Words and Music by
PRINCE

KISS

Words and Music by
PRINCE

146

U GOT THE LOOK

Words and Music by
PRINCE

Medium Dance groove

(Whispered:) Here we are, folks,   the dream we all dream of:

boy versus girl,

*Recorded a half step higher.

HOT THING

Words and Music by
PRINCE

Moderately

Recorded a half step higher.

156

I can't wait 2 get U home, _ where we can be a-

lone. _ Hot thing, _ I could read U po - e - try _ and then

we could make a sto - ry of our own.

Hot thing.

THIEVES IN THE TEMPLE

Words and Music by
PRINCE

CREAM

Words and Music by
PRINCE

This is it.

It's time 4 U 2 go 2 the wi - - re.
ba - by, there ain't no - bod - y bet - - ter.
why should U wait an - y long - - er?